Look for Them:
Where Are the Shapes?

by Donna Loughran

Content Consultant
David T. Hughes
Mathematics Curriculum Specialist

NORWOOD HOUSE PRESS
Chicago, IL

Norwood House Press
PO Box 316598
Chicago, IL 60631

For information regarding Norwood House Press, please visit our website at
www.norwoodhousepress.com or call 866-565-2900.

Special thanks to: Heidi Doyle
Production Management: Six Red Marbles
Editors: Linda Bullock and Kendra Muntz
Printed in Heshan City, Guangdong, China. 208N—012013

Library of Congress Cataloging–in-Publication Data

Loughran, Donna.

Look for them: where are the shapes? / by Donna Loughran; consultant
David Hughes, mathematics curriculum specialist.
p. cm.—(iMath)

Audience: 6–8.
Audience: K to Grade 3.
Summary: "The mathematical concepts of shapes, sizes, and colors are
introduced as students explore a local playground. As the students identify
attributes of objects, they also learn about flat and three-dimensional
shapes, prepositions, and art materials such as clay, tissue paper, and
paint. This book includes a discovery activity, an art connection, and
mathematical vocabulary introduction"—Provided by publisher.

Includes bibliographical references and index.

ISBN: 978-1-59953-550-0 (library edition: alk. paper)
ISBN: 978-1-60357-519-5 (ebook)

1. Geometry—Juvenile literature. I. Title.

QA445.5.L68 2013
516'.15—dc23
2012031017

CONTENTS

Note to Caregivers:

Throughout this book, many questions are posed to the reader. Some are open-ended and ask what the reader thinks. Discuss these questions with your child and guide him or her in thinking through the possible answers and outcomes. There are also questions posed which have a specific answer. Encourage your child to read through the text to determine the correct answer. Most importantly, encourage answers grounded in reality while also allowing imaginations to soar. Information to help support you as you share the book with your child is provided in the back in the **Additional Notes** section.

Bold words are defined in the glossary in the back of the book.

4

What Do You See?

"Look up. Look down. Look all around. What shapes do you see?" Mrs. Fox asked.

Laura pointed up. "I see **rectangles**," she said.

Brian pointed to the floor. "I see **squares**," he said.

Ana pointed to the clock. "I see a **circle**," she said.

Mrs. Fox clapped her hands. "Good," she said. "You found rectangles, squares, and circles. Does anyone see a **triangle**?"

Matt pointed to the wall. "There are strings of triangles!" he called out.

Mrs. Fox clapped her hands again. "Yes! There are shapes all around us."

Write down a list of words that describe each shape.

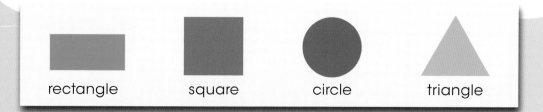

rectangle   square   circle   triangle

Mrs. Fox challenged the class. "We found many flat shapes in the room. Do you see any shapes that are not flat?"

Toni tossed a ball. "This is a **sphere**."

Marty held up a box of tissues. "This is a **cube**."

Ricky pointed to the jar of flowers on Mrs. Fox's desk. "The flowers are in a **cylinder**."

sphere

cube

cylinder

"And there are some **cones**!" called Mia. She pointed to tops of colored pencils.

Write down a list of words that describe each shape.

cone

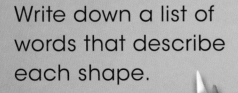

What Shapes Do You See?

"You did very well," said Mrs. Fox. "I think you are ready for a surprise."

"You are going to need some paper and crayons. We are going to look for shapes outside. Then, I have some ideas for making artwork with these shapes."

Idea 1: "You can use colorful paper to make and place shapes," said Mrs. Fox. "You cut shapes from paper.

Then, you glue them to another piece of paper to make a **collage**." Mrs. Fox held up a collage for everyone to see.

Do you think making a collage is a good way to make and place shapes? Why or why not?

Idea 2: "You can use **paint** to make and place shapes on paper," Mrs. Fox explained.

Do you think painting is a good way to make and place shapes? Why or why not?

Idea 3: "You can use **clay** or objects to build and place shapes," said Mrs. Fox.

Do you think building is a good way to make and place shapes? Why or why not?

Discover Activity

Materials
- paper
- crayons

Do You See What I See?

Draw a shape picture.
Use different shapes. Color them different colors. Put shapes in different places.

Then, ask your friends or family to play a game with you. Give each player a piece of paper and some crayons.

Use words to describe what is in your picture. Give shapes names. Describe colors. Tell them where shapes are. For example, there might be a blue square behind a yellow circle.

Give everyone time to draw what you described. Then, compare pictures. Do they look alike? Did you explain your picture well?

Shapes Are Everywhere

"Are we ready?" asked Mrs. Fox.

Everyone nodded yes.

"Good. Stay with me and remember to keep your eyes open. Let's all look for shapes. Call out when you see something. Then, we can draw them to remember them."

"I see some shapes," called Thomas. He pointed to a hopscotch drawing on the ground.

What shape is repeated in the drawing?

What number is above 1?

What number is next to 3?

What numbers are below 8? How many shapes can you find in the drawing?

Look What's Spinning

"Look," Jax told everyone. "Do you see that girl?"

"Yes," Mrs. Fox answered. "It looks like she is having fun. She is spinning a hoop round and round. Has anyone else tried that?"

Almost everyone raised a hand. "We play games with hoops in gym class," said Madison.

"And my friends and I have contests to see who can spin the longest," said Jaime.

What shape is a hoop?

What color hoop is the girl spinning?

What color hoop is around her feet?

Toss It

"Let's keep walking," Mrs. Fox said, leading the class forward.

Nearby, a boy tossed a huge red ball into the air. "Look, class," said Mrs. Fox. "Doesn't that look like fun?"

"Catch it! Catch it!" Noah called to the boy. And the boy did.

What shape is the ball?

What color is it?

Is the ball above or below the boy's hands?

Are the trees behind or in front of the boy?

Road Sign Ahead

"Mrs. Fox," Abby called. "We can visit the children's playground across the street. There are lots of shapes there."

"That's a good idea," said Mrs. Fox. "We'll have to cross the road carefully. Follow me, children."

Mrs. Fox led the class across the street. When everyone was on the sidewalk, Mrs. Fox pointed to a sign at the end of the road.

"What do you see there?" she asked the class.

What shape is the sign?

What shapes are inside the sign?

What color is the shape above the yellow shape?

What color is the shape below the yellow shape?

On the Playground

"Abby," said Mrs. Fox, "your idea was wonderful. Look at all of the shapes around us."

"Look!" Kylie said excitedly. She ran to a group of plastic shapes near where the youngest children play.

"Wow!" exclaimed Mrs. Fox. "Those shapes are fantastic! I'm going to draw one of each thing I see."

What is the green shape with the pointed top called?

What is the red shape beside the green pointed shape?

What is the blue shape behind the green pointed shape?

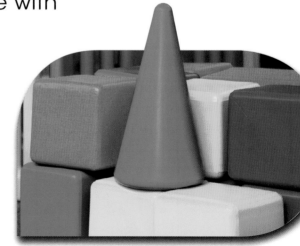

Back to Class

Mrs. Fox led the class around the playground. They walked across the playing fields. And they visited the pond behind the middle school.

"There really are shapes all around us," said Noah. He used a stick to make shapes in the water.

Ella stood next to Noah. "I have drawn lots of shapes. They are all different sizes. And they are different shapes, too."

"Good," said Mrs. Fox. "Those shapes will give you lots of ideas for your art project."

"Your drawings are wonderful! It's time to go back to class now. We have some art to make!"

The children hurried back. They were eager to get started.

Connecting to Art

Before the children began working, Mrs. Fox shared a picture with them. "This," she said, "is a **mosaic** [moh-ZAY-ik]. It is made of pieces of tile. Each piece has a shape and a color."

"Artists have made mosaics for many, many years. You can see them on walls and buildings."

"Sometimes, a mosaic makes a picture. Sometimes, we don't see a picture in the mosaic. Instead, we see a collection of shapes."

What shapes do you see in this mosaic?

Math at Work

Some artists make art for the outdoors. A gardener used flowerpots to make outdoor art. She drew a design. Then, she figured out what she needed.

How many pots did the gardener use in all?

How many medium pots did the gardener use in all?

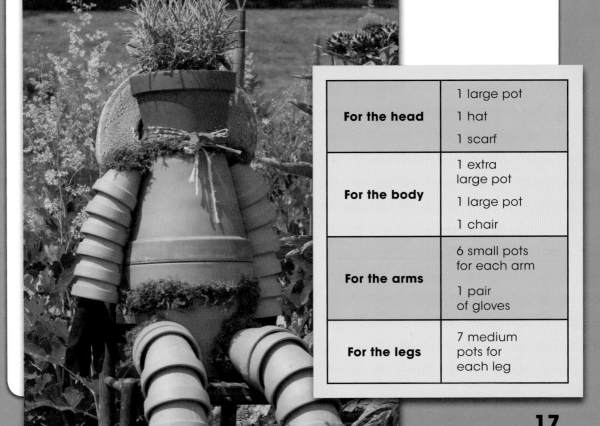

For the head	1 large pot
	1 hat
	1 scarf
For the body	1 extra large pot
	1 large pot
	1 chair
For the arms	6 small pots for each arm
	1 pair of gloves
For the legs	7 medium pots for each leg

A Museum in the Classroom

The children made an art museum in their classroom. They taped their drawings on the walls. Then, they walked around the room to look at each drawing carefully.

The drawings showed colorful shapes. There were squares, rectangles, triangles, and circles. There were cubes, cones, cylinders, and spheres. Some drawings showed real things, like birds and clouds.

In some drawings, the shapes went across the page. In other drawings, the shapes went up and down. There were also drawings with shapes that went sideways.

"Now, class. Are you ready to use shapes to make more art?" asked Mrs. Fox.

The children nodded their heads. They were eager to begin.

"Think about how you will make shapes," said Mrs. Fox.

Idea 1: "You can cut shapes from paper. Then, you glue the shapes to a large sheet of paper to make a **collage**. A collage is a wonderful way to show shapes. But cutting lots of shapes takes time."

Idea 2: "Or you can use **paint** to make and place shapes on paper. Painting is fun. But it can be messy, too. If you decide to paint, be sure you put on your art smocks first."

Idea 3: "Or you can use **clay** or objects to build shapes. You need to know what materials you want to use. Will you use clay? Will you use cardboard? How will you put the pieces together? Make a plan before you begin building," said Mrs. Fox.

Soon, everyone was hard at work. Colorful shapes began to appear. Many were small. Others were huge! The new art projects were going to be great!

What Comes Next?

Design a piece of art for a garden. Follow these steps.

1. Choose a place in the garden to put the art.
2. Choose the materials you will use.
3. Choose the shapes you will use.
4. Decide what size to make each shape.
5. Decide how you will arrange each shape. Will some shapes go up and down? Will some go sideways? Will others go in a different direction?
6. Pick the materials you will use to make the art.
7. Draw a picture of the art you will make.

Ask an adult to help you make it. Then, put it outdoors so others can see it, too.

GLOSSARY

circle: a flat, perfectly round shape.

clay: a material that can be molded into different forms.

collage: a piece of art made by gluing different materials to a flat surface.

cones: solid shapes with a circle for a base and a point at the top.

cube: a solid shape with six square sides.

cylinder: a solid shape with a circle at the top and the bottom.

mosaic: a picture made using pieces of tile. The tile is different shapes and colors.

paint: a material used to create art. It comes in many colors.

rectangles: flat shapes with four sides.

sphere: a solid circle that forms a globe shape.

square: flat shapes with four sides of equal length.

triangle: a flat shape with three sides.

FURTHER READING

FICTION

Mouse Shapes, by Ellen Stoll Walsh, Harcourt Children's Books, 2007

Round Is a Mooncake: A Book of Shapes, by Roseanne Thong, Chronicle Books, 2000

NONFICTION

The Shape Song Swingalong, by Steve Songs, Barefoot Books, 2011

3-D Shapes, by Marina Cohen, Crabtree Publishing Company, 2010

Additional Notes

The page references below provide answers to questions asked throughout the book. Questions whose answers will vary are not addressed.

Page 10: Squares are repeated in the drawing. The number 2 is above the number 1. The number 4 is next to the number 3. The numbers 6 and 7 are below the number 8.

Page 11: The hoop is a circle. The girl is spinning a blue hoop. There is a purple hoop around the girl's feet.

Page 12: The ball is a sphere. The ball is red. The ball is above the boy's hands. The trees are behind the boy.

Page 13: The sign is a triangle. Circles are inside the sign. There is a red circle above the yellow circle. There is a green circle below the yellow circle.

Page 14: The green shape with the pointed top is a cone. The red shape beside the cone is a cube. The blue shape behind the cone is a cube.

Page 17: The gardener used 29 pots in all. The gardener used 7 medium pots on each leg, for a total of 14 medium pots.

Index

Content Consultant

David T. Hughes

David is an experienced mathematics teacher, writer, presenter, and adviser. He serves as a consultant for the Partnership for Assessment of Readiness for College and Careers. David has also worked as the Senior Program Coordinator for the Charles A. Dana Center at The University of Texas at Austin and was an editor and contributor for the *Mathematics Standards in the Classroom* series.